Bibliographic information published by the German National Library:

The German National Library lists this publication in the National Bibliography; detailed bibliographic data are available on the Internet at http://dnb.dnb.de .

Imprint:

Copyright © 2006 GRIN Verlag, Open Publishing GmbH
Print and binding: Books on Demand GmbH, Norderstedt Germany
ISBN: 9783656872924

This book at GRIN:

http://www.grin.com/en/e-book/115491/the-story-of-black-elk-as-fiction-and-bio-graphy-black-elk-speaks-by

Martin Setzkorn

The story of Black Elk as fiction and biography. „Black Elk speaks" by John G. Neihardt versus "The heartsong of Charging Elk" by James Welch

GRIN Publishing

GRIN - Your knowledge has value

Since its foundation in 1998, GRIN has specialized in publishing academic texts by students, college teachers and other academics as e-book and printed book. The website www.grin.com is an ideal platform for presenting term papers, final papers, scientific essays, dissertations and specialist books.

Universität Rostock

Institut für Anglistik/Amerikanistik

Comparison

„The heartsong of Charging Elk" – „Black Elk speaks"

Martin Setzkorn

List of contents

1 Introduction

In this paper I am going to compare the authobiography "Black Elk speaks" written by John G. Neihardt with the novel "The heartsong of Charging Elk" written by James Welch. Both books show a different perspective on the same topic. "Black Elk speaks" shows the true history whereas the novel from James Welch is fiction. But by reading both books I got the impression that even "The heartsong of Charging Elk" could have really happened. By reading the books a lot of connections or links get obvious.

The paper tries to discuss some of the connections. In the first part of the paper the stories will be summarized and the main characters Black Elk and Charging Elk will be described. In the center part of the paper some of the connections and links will be compared more detailed. Here I will triy to point out especially the connections they have during their travel to Europe.

In the last part I am going to discuss the interesting changes of the narrative perspective and the resulting impression for the reader.

2 Characterization and appearances of the main characters

Both characters raise difficulties in their descriptions. The influence of the dramatical changes of their homelands have impacts on them. The characters change over time probably more than it used to have without these changes.

2.1 Charging Elk

Charging Elk is a beloved son. His father and mother are Oglala Indians. His sister and his brother died in the struggle with the white men.

Charging Elk is described as a tall, strong man and has the typical stereotyped Indian appearance that contents the dark skin color whereas his own is even darker than the usual skin color of the other Indians. The Indians even picked on him about that fact but his mother told him that he was the purest. That's why he is darker than the others. The long and dark hair means a lot to him.

His appearance is even more outstanding from the *wasichu*[1] point of view. From the wasichu sight not only his skin color, his dark long hair and his dark eyes make him to someone different. He is described that way:

"He was at least four hands taller than the tallest of them ..." (Welch, 2001, p.12)

His character is dominated by friendliness. Other characters in the book describe him as patient and with good will. The reader gets the impression that these normally good charactertraits are sometimes misplaced. That is one of the reasons why he sometimes has trouble to figure out who is a friend and who is an enemy. It seems that the more the people get to know him the more they rely on him and see him as a good friend.

He loves the nature and the animals and is very proud of his horse "High Runner".

It is easy to see that he is changing during the novel getting more and more responsible for him and others.

2.2 Black Elk

Black Elk is unlike Charging Elk not really described from other perspectives. If he talks about himself he mostly describes his age and how early he had to be a grown up. So the picture of him I am going to describe is more or less grown by reading his story.

He is an Lakota Indian and believes strong in the Indian spirit. It seems that his life is dominated by his visions and the power he takes out of the visions. But a second point has much influence on his character. That is the continually loss of his motherland. He constantly tries to stop the retreat and is always searching for a way to get the life back his parents used to live and he lived when he was a young boy. At first it seems that because of his visions he is a

---

[1] Wasichu: A term used to designate the white man, but having no reference to the color of his skin.

loner. But later because of the power he takes out of the visions he is more and more respected and integrated in the Indian community.

3 Summary of the stories

3.1 "The heartsong of Charging Elk"

The novel describes the life of an Lakota Indian starting out in his homeland. Still when he was a boy he had to move in with his parents to live at the Red Cloud Agency. Later they moved to the Pine Ridge Agency. When he was thirteen years old he left with his friend Strikes Plenty the agency to live at Whirlwind Compound. There he lived far from the agency and from school. They had constantly to retreat because of the wasichus who took more and more over their place. He was forced to live in the badlands in a place called Stronghold. This place could be easily defended and the white men, soldiers and settlers were afraid of the Indians who lived out there. Charging Elk stayed there for nine years. Learning the so called old ways of hunting and exploring tought by two old medicine men. These years had a formative influence on him. The life out there was getting more and more difficult. The changes which resulted out of the wasichu dominance forced him to go back to the agency. Otherwise, especially in the winters, it was really hard to survive.

Everything changes when scouts from the Buffalo Bill Show make a contest in the agency where he has to ride and fight on his horse "High Runner". He is chosen for the Show because of his perfect Indian skills and his perfect Indian appearance.

Now for him starts a new adventure with a travel to Europe. In Europe he works in the Buffalo Bill Show until he gets lost and has to live in a country where he is not only a foreigner but also outstanding because of the fact that he looks totally different than anybody else and is not able to talk their language, and nobody speaks his language. He starts to live there at first with the aim to return. During his days in Europe he is searching more and more for a wife and a family. By trying to achieve the second point it seems that achieving the first point gets more and more difficult. In the end he has the opportunity to go back but he decides to stay with his wife and unborn child in Europe. But during all that time he never forgets and always is reminded especially in bad times of his past life. His dreams and visions are with him all the time.

3.2 "Black Elk speaks"

Black Elk was born as an Oglala Indian araound 1860 at a place that is now the Pine Ridge Reservation. His life is dominated already when he is a little boy by visions. He received the first vision with the age of five. Most of his life he tries to figure out what he has to do with the knowlege he had through the visions. Because of the changing time and the loss of his homeland his childhod is very short. He has early to do the work of a grown up and has to fight already as a boy against the wasichus He receives more visions which are even more powerful. These visions make him capable to help other sick Indians. As a boy he believed that everybody would think he is crazy if he had talked about the visions but later the Indians believe in him and his visions. With fourteen years he and his community surrendered to the wasichus to escape starvation. In that winter in the same agency were Black Elk stayed they killed the great chief Crazy Horse. This had an big influence on the Indians. Many escaped like Black Elk an tried to start a new life in the lands they used to live. Black Elks power was growing stronger in that time and is more and more useful for his people. He receives new visions and with the help of a medicine man he understands more and more what the visions want him to do.

The wasichus slaughtered the last bisons. And most of the Indians also Black Elk, now twenty years old, had to settle down in square gray houses. The circle of life the Indians used to live was broken when the bison herds didn´t arrive as usually. In that time he continued curring the sick. Three years later he goes with the Buffelo Bill show first to Omaha, Chicago and New York and then he crosses the Atlantic and performs in Europe. In Europe he loses all his indian power. After a wihle he gets lost but togetheter with other Indians he manages to get to another show. In that time he has a spirit journey while he is sick . After recovering Pahuska the show leader gives him the money to return back to Pine Ridge. Here he finds his power again and is involved in a side fight of Wounded Knee. A few days after the massacre at Wounded Knee he surrenders with his people the second time to escape starvation.

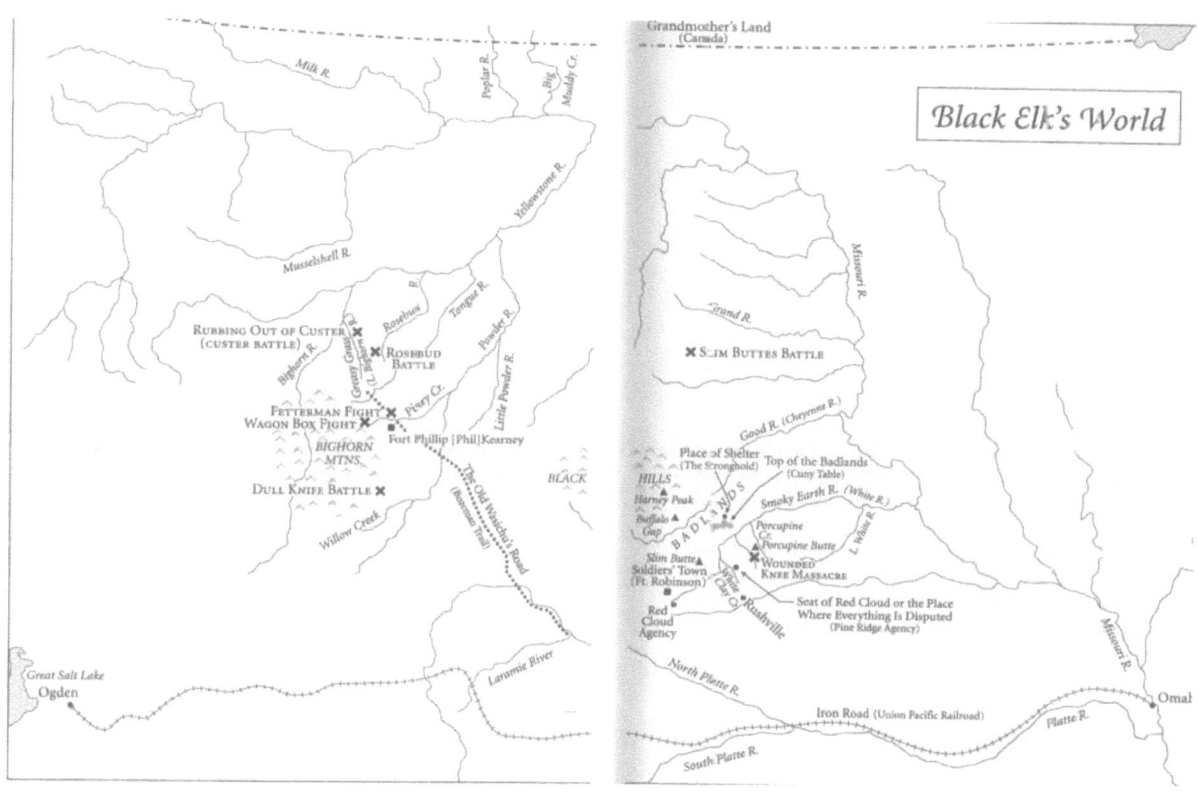

(Neihardt, 2004)

4 Links between the books

There are many different links between the books. This is already very obvious by looking at the changing settings in the books. Both main characters have nearly the same childhood, growing up between the agency and the badlands. At that time they learn the Indian way of life. They learn how to survive in nature. In the next lines I give a short overview about the most important links and conections.

Overview about linking points:
- the Names: Charging **Elk** – Black **Elk**

- they belong to the same tribe **Oglalas**
- they believe in **Wakan Tanka**
- they **grow up** at the **same places**
- they **fight** against the **wasichus**
- they **drop Shool** after a short time
- they have only three years differences in their **age**
- they both go with the **Buffalo Bill Show** to **Europe**
- they **get lost** in Europe
- they **live in a foreign family** for a while
- they have **visions**
- they have **spirit journeys**

There are a lot more facts which are connecting the two texts. But already these facts show how on one side the texts are closely linked. On the other side the stories are totally different. It is very interesting to get knowlege of happenings at that time, for example Wounded Knee, from different perspectives. Both stories start out pretty much the same way and end in different directions.

Some connections are compared in point five more detailed.

5 Connections between the two texts especially connections in the travel to Europe

5.1 Atlantic as a border

For Charging Elk and Black Elk the European experience starts with the crossing of the Atlantic. They leave their well known home country to see the home country of the wasichus. Both believe if they learn how the wasichu world functions it would be useful knowledge in the fight against the wasichus to save their homeland as they used to know it when they were young. Black Elk believes already by crossing the border that he will not make it. Like most of the Indians he is getting sea sick and probably because of the fact that he is so helpless being just a passenger on the fire boat he believes his end is near.

Black Elk: "*I dressed for death, putting on my best clothes that I wore in the show, and then I sang my death song.*"(Neihardt, 2004, p.168)

Charging Elk makes the same experience. He also believes that he is not able to survive the crossing.

Charging Elk: "*The fire boat had crashed up and down and rolled from side to side and he had become sick almost instantly after losing sight of the big town*" (Welch, 2001, p.61)

The reader gets the impression that both characters are helpless already during the travel in the other world. It seems that without the help of the wasichus they are not able to cross the border themselves. This way of thinking changes after knowing the fact that both cross the Atlantic by themselves in the so called spirit journey and there it seems very easy for them. Charging Elk crosses the border physically only once and decides to stay in the European world whereas Black Elk decides to go back and live in his home country again. One reason for this decision is that he does not feel his power which he received through the visions

Black Elk: *All the time I was away from the home across the big water, my power was gone, and I was like a dead man moving around most of the time* (Neihardt, 2004, p.178).

The difficulties of the crossing symbolize that it is not easy to cross the border between the two different worlds. Not only physical problems but also all the differences in life like language and culture which occur in the European world are for both characters hard to overcome.

5.2 Death song

The death song is very important for the Indians. Black Elk and Charging Elk learned already the death songs when they were children. It is not only used by fighting enemies but also in situations where death is near or around. The Indians believe that if they die they all meet again in another place. Especially men have to be brave so that their naki (soul) could cross over to their already died relatives.

It was interesting to see that both characters have similar situations in which they use their death song. Especially in fight situations the death song seems to be very helpful.

For both the first time they sing their death song is during the crossing to Europe. There they dress up in best clothes and start to sing their death song. Charging Elk has a lot of situations in Europe where he feels helpless or even lonesome. For example in prison he even hopes to die.

Charging Elk:" *For two days, Charging Elk had lain on the sleeping platform and sung his death song. It was a powerful song and it took him away to his own country.* " (Welch, 2001, p.104)

From Charging Elks point of view this singing of the death song is the escape from prison.

Charging Elk: *"He did not feel the cold or see the close stone walls.* "(Welch, 2001, p.104)

In that situation Charging Elk is described in the book by Martin St-Cyr's as a dying animal:

Martin St-Cyr's: *"They were the eyes of a dying animal, of an animal that had resigned itself to death."* (Welch, 2001, p.103)

10

A second situation where Charging Elk uses his death song is a fighting situation. One night in a bar he gets in trouble with sailors. There is no easy way out and so he starts singing his death song in believe that this is his last fight. After escaping the situation he thinks back and he feels very strong. In the book it is described.

Charging Elk: *"He had remembered that he was a man, and a man who sings his death song in a proper way is a man to be reckoned with."*(Welch, 2001, p.202)

Black Elk uses his death song in the same way as Charging Elk. The only difference is that sometimes in fighting situations he sings different songs to get courage to fight the enemy. One fighting song he starts with the following sentence and then starts to fight:

Black Elk: *"Take courage. These are our relatives. We will try to get them back." Then we all sang a song* ...(Neihardt, 2004, p.198)

The reason why Black Elk uses different songs is probably because of the fact that he sings together with other Indians whereas Charging Elk is always alone in fearful situations.

5.3 The Buffalo Bill Show

For both characters the show gives them the opportunity to get to know the motherland of the enemy but also the chance to escape from their home country which is in a change right now. That means that through the conquest of the wasichus the circle of life they use to know starves.

It is weird that the wasichus who do everything to destroy the Indians world and the way they used to live pay them so that they show in the Buffalo Bill Show their life as they used to live it. The opportunity the show offers is not for every Indian. You have to be the stereotype Indian. Charging Elk and Black

Elk have two facts which are important to be a part in the show. Both have perfect Indian skills in riding and fighting and have the typical Indian appearance.

BUFFALO BILL TO THE RESCUE.

(White, 1994, p.52)

Both characters leave their home countries with the strong believe that they only go for a limited time. That would have probably be the case if they had both stayed in the show all the time. But through incident both get lost and have to manage their life in the foreign world without the show.

By reading the stories the most important thing about the show is that it gives the opportunity to go to Europe and maybe the even more important opportunity to leave Europe.

After getting lost the characters struggle with the European life until they met up again with the show. So the Buffalo Bill Show is framing the European travel. Black Elk takes the chance to leave Europe after four years whereas Charging Elk decides after sixteen years to stay in Europe when he is offered a ticket to go home.

Black Elk: *Then he asked me if I wanted to be in the show or if I wanted to go home. I told him I was sick to go home.* (Neihardt, 2004, p.175)

Charging Elk: *This is my home now, Joseph. I have a wife. Soon I will have a child, the Moon of Frost in the Tipi.* (Welch, 2001, p.437)

Another linking fact in the novel written by James Welch is that both characters not only know each other but also meet. They grew up together but Black Elk is three years older than Charging Elk and that is why each one played with his own peer group. While Charging Elk is at the Buffalo Bill Show Black Elk returns to the show. The returning of Black Elk is well described from Charging Elks point of view.

It is interesting that James Welch tries to write the story about an Indian with a true history. That is what Arnold Krupat describes in his book "Red Matters" when he talks about "Black Elk speaks". On the one sight he says that there are non-chronological anecdotes full of mystical happenings but Elk is still true history. (Krupat, 2002)

5.4 The visions and spirit journeys

The visions are very important to the Indians. It seems that they need the visions to get to know what they live for. One major rule of visions is that you never tell anybody the hole vision you received. Visions are responsible for the spiritual power an Indian has. Through the visions they find out which powers are helpful for them. Michae E. Staub believes that visions even if they are told with lot of details can never replace the fact of receiving a vision.

The limits of writing and reading are here dramatized. No reader can "see" because speech demands presence, and no text can create a living voice, and so, like "Black Elk speaks",..., asserts the spoken word's primacy over writing. (Staub, 1994)

In contrast to the quotation of Michael E. Staub it is interesting to mention that for example in a movie like "Hidalgo" visions are shown with real voices and moving pictures. In this film the vision occurs close to the end and gives the Indian the strength to finish the horse race.

Black Elk had already when he was a young boy at the age of five strong visions. The power he had grew stronger with every vision he received. Charging Elk had also visions as a young boy. Neither one of them has a vision during the stay in Europe. They try to remember of their visions but they feel powerless. When Black Elk returns from Europe his power comes back and through other visions he gets even more power than before.

But both characters have a spiritual journey when they are in Europe. They are travelling easily back to their home country and see their people from above. They are actually flying on a cloud and see their real life in their home world. Black Elk sees only a normal day but gets really home sick because of the fact that he sees his mother. He wants to communicate with her but he can only look at her, there is no way of communication.

Charging Elk makes the same journey as Black Elk. But when he arrives he sees his people at Wounded Knee. And there he is a witness of the massacre of Wounded Knee. He tries to jump of the imaginary cliff he is on to join his people. But he always is blown back and a voice is talking to him which says:

Charging Elk: *You are my only son.*(Welch, 2001, p.235)

Later close to the end of the story he is told that the voice belongs to his mother.

Whereas the visions always give them power the spirit journeys weaken them.

5.5 The Massacre at Wounded Knee

The massacre at Wounded Knee happened in December the 29th in 1890 in South Dakota.

The great chief Big Foot was coming down from the Badlands with nearly 400 people. There were only about hundred warriors in this band. All the others were women , children and old men. They surrendered and went along with the soldiers to Wounded Knee Creek. While the soldiers were searching all the Tepees for weapons through an incident a gun went off. After that the soldiers opened the fire and killed everybody.

Both go through the experience of Wounded Knee in different ways.
Black Elk had already returned from his trip to Europe. He was located fifteen miles away from Wounded Knee. When he arrives at Wounded Knee he is involved in some smaller fights around Wounded Knee Creek. Later that day he arrives at Wounded Knee Creek and describes it this way.

Black Elk: *When I saw this I wished that I had died too, but I was not sorry for the women and children. It was better for them to be happy in the other world and I wanted to be there too. But before I went there I wanted to help revenge. I thought there might be a day, and we should have revenge.* (Neihardt, 2004, p.200)

In the story this massacre describes the end of the Indian life Black Elk used to know. He wants revenge but realizes the situation and surrenders. He finishes the story with the words

Black Elk*: There is no center any longer, and the sacred tree is dead* (Neihardt, 2004, p.207).

In the book "American Indian Literature. An Anthology" edited by Alan R. Velie John Neihardt comments to his own book "Black Elk speaks" that Black Elk correctives the picture which uses to have known about the battles between the Indians and the soldiers (Neihardt, 1991).

Charging Elk is not physically there. But in his spirit journey he looks down at his people and sees the same as Black Elk saw.

Charging Elk: *...he looked down and he saw his people lying in a heap at the bottom. They lay in all positions and directions – men, women and children even old ones. They lay like buffaloes that had been driven over the cliffs by hunters,...* (Welch, 2001, p.235)

In the book it is described that he has the feeling that it is not a spirit journey or dream but he has been there. Even thinking about the fact that Charging Elk is thousand of miles away and he does not know exactly what happened it has a big influence on him.

Both characters have knowledge about the happenings but can not do anything to change the situation or to take revenge for the killed Indians.

6 Narrative perspectives and the impression on the reader

The narrative perspective changes in both books for different reasons. In "Black Elk speaks" most of the time Black Elk speaks himself. But when he describes different situations the reader gets the impression that he does not get to know all the facts. For example when Black Elk was a little boy a lot of fighting between his tribe and the wasichus happened. In that time he only describes that his father and other Indians went of to fight. He was to small for fighting so he had to stay home. Now somebody else, for example Five Thunder, Standing Bear or Iron Hawk, take over. The situations are told from another perspective again. The reader has the impression that the angle of his view opens up a lot with the change of the narrative perspective in "Black Elk speaks".

In "The heartsong of Charging Elk" the change of the perspectives has the same influence on the reader like in "Black Elk speaks". The angle of knowledge opens a lot by the changes between the narrators. But here a different situations is present. The reader gets to know facts which even Charging Elk does not know. For example in Europe when people are talking Charging Elk can not understand what they talk. So from his perspective we only get to know what he understands out of their talking. Mostly these are only words like "Indian" or "Buffalo Bill Show' he recognizes but he can not make out the meaning. Now The persepctive changes and the reader gets the knowledge what the others are talking about.

Other situations are situations when Charging Elk is in prison. He can rot tlak about the story anymore because of the fact that he does not know what is going on. Now the perspective is changing to somebody outside the prison and the reader gets to know a lot more than Charging Elk.

The reader always has all persepective. He sees the situations through the eyes of Charging Elk and he gets to know how different characters look at Charging Elk. So the reader does not only get to know what their are talking about but also how Charging Elk and the charcters ffel in different situations.

For example in some situations Charging Elk wants to tell the outside something and the outside wants to tell him exactly the same thing but they can not understand each other. Because of that Charging Elk often gets in trouble just because of the missing opportunity of communication.

But sometimes is the other way around. For example when he is in a bar sailors are starting trouble with him and because of the fact that he can not understand them he believes a long time that their are friends.

This struggle of communicaton is really good shown and very interesting for the reader.

This way of narration is easy to manage because of the fact that it is in contrast to "Black Elk speaks" not an authobiography but a novel.

The changing angles in the books give the reader the impression of an objective picture.

7 Conclusion

By comparing the two books it is visible that they have a lot in common.

This is already underlindes by comparing the characterizations. Here are nearly two equal characters shown. Another connection is given if you look at the main frame of ths stories. If the reader would only know these facts it could appear the thinking that you have only to read one of the two books. But in a closer comparison there appear a lot of differences. After having compared both books I would say that the books complement one another to show a more detailed picture of the happenings. One of the biggest differences is the ending of each story. One character decides to go back and the other stays in the new world. Another interesting point was that I had the impression that not only Black Elk but also Charging Elk could have been a real story. But the changing narrative perspectives would in a true story probably not be possible. Both books show the innocence of the Indians which is described also by Michael E: Staub:

What almost destroys the Sioux people is their innocent acceptance of the promises made by "the gnawing flood of the Wasichus" who were "dirty with lies and greed". (Staub, 1994, p.62)

Literature

- **Krupat, A.(2002):** *Red matters. Native American Studies.* Pennsylvania: University of Pennsylvania Press.

- **Neihardt, J.G.(2004):** *Black Elk speaks.* Nebraska: University of Nebraska Press.

- **Neihardt, J.G.(1991):** *Black Elk speaks by John G. Neihardt.* in: Velie, A.R.: American Indian Literature. An Anthology. Oklahoma: University of Oklahoma Press.

- **Staub, M.E.(1994):** *Voices of persuasion. Politics of presentation in 1930s America.* Cambridge: Cambridge University Press.

- **Welch, J.(2001):** *The heartsong of Charging Elk.* New York: Anchor Books.

- **White, R.(1994):** *Frederick Jackson Turner and Buffalo Bill.* In: Grossman, J.R.: The frontier in american culture. Berkeley, Los Angelos: University of California Press.